HEY YOU, IT'S ME

BY

MELANIE ARMSTRONG

Watching your children grow up is like watching dawn break over an endless horizon—each day a new, radiant possibility. In their laughter, their dreams, and even their struggles, you witness a journey of wonder.

Illustrated by Kathleen Andrews

Copyright ©2024 Melanie Armstrong

All rights reserved.

No part of this book may be reproduced or transmitted in any form or by any means, electronic or mechanical, including photocopying, recording, or by any information storage and retrieval system, without written permission from the author. The story, all names, characters, and incidents portrayed in this production are fictitious. No identification with actual persons (living or deceased), places, buildings, and products is intended or should be inferred.

Illustrated by Kathleen Andrews

Paperback ISBN: 979-8-895-90035-2

Hardcover ISBN: 979-8-218-51266-8

ACKNOWLEDGMENTS

To all those who pick up this book, thank you for giving my words a chance. Noah and Avery, I dedicate this book to you. You both have taught me more about myself than you could ever imagine. The one important gift you have shown me through your life is that milestones do not stop at any age. Life is beautiful in such a delicate way that if we pause and be present, we will see a sense of renewal and growth at all milestones along the way in our lives. I also dedicate this to Warren my husband, confidant, my love, and most of all my very best friend. Kathleen thank you for your beautiful illustrations and guidance through this book. Your vision and artistic talent is incredible and spot on. Lastly, thank you to the Sunchasers who were there before motherhood, during and always. I will never forget the reading circle on the lake that inspired this book, especially Kelly Kirkham Flint who continued to help guide the vision of this book in the right direction. Sunchaser's unite!

Hey you...
It's me, as close as I can be.
Looking through the lens
of what I used to see.

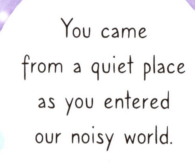

You came
from a quiet place
as you entered
our noisy world.

Your eyes
circled around,
fingers and toes
swayed and swirled.

Your first smile, first giggle,
your beautiful face glows and beams.

Like rainbows
spilling into our world,
weaving all through our dreams.

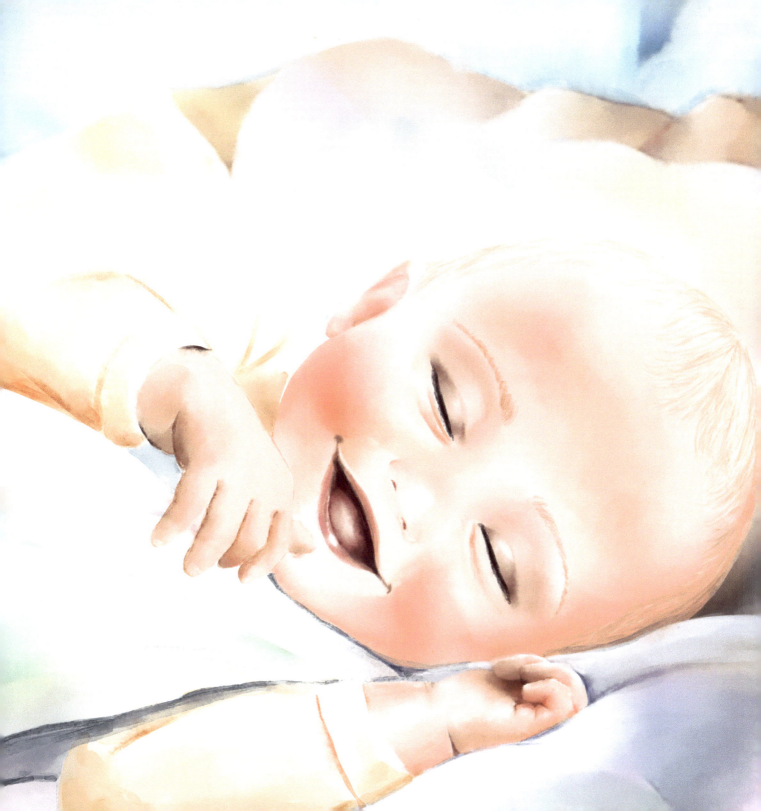

Hey you, my tiny crawler.
I am close as I can be.

Destined to fill your world
with magical possibilities.

Watching you as you grow and conquer challenging heights.
Taking risks as you explore all new sounds and sights.
Blushing as you giggle, running to and from my arms.

Practice. Makes. Perfect.

Hey you, my little mini me,
I am close as I can be,
even in the moments
we're not together physically.

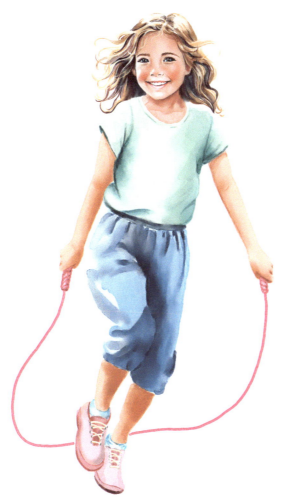

Those seemingly forever moments when I had to be away
My heart simply ached to make sure you were happy and okay.

I arrive after being gone, I see you jumping on our street.
Our eyes met, two hearts connect.
Our love, our time did not skip a beat...

Hey you,
my young child,
I am close as I can be.
watching you embark
this world with curiosity.

A quiet space,
a warm place in my heart.
Memories
of how you've grown.

Our very first
handheld walk to school,
somehow I've always known.

I knew that you were special,
I knew that you were kind.
You had the strength
to take risks
then reflect
in your beautiful mind.

Hey you, my little adventurer
it is me,
as close as I can be.

Giving you space
giving you time

Go out, go do, go see.

In your little years I saw your enthusiasm grow
Your energy unbounded
Always on the go.

You spoke your heart, your voice was loud
Your words were very clear
Your energy so magnetic
Friends gather as I spied from the rear

Hey you, my beautiful teen
I am close as I can be,
giving space,
giving grace.
Your brief escape from me.

Peaceful moments
as you began to reflect.
Your big bright eyes gleamed
as your dreams began to collect.

Collecting courage and strength
when you fell and stumbled.
Collecting grace through hardships,
you were ever so humbled.

Encouraging friendships that loved and sometimes hurt.
You danced with strangers,
your whimsical moves and delicate flirts.

Yes my love, I am here as close as I can be,
watching you embrace the world so independently.

Mimicking new facial expressions,
you morphed a whole new look,

I watched you from afar
write your own story book.

Learning from friends,
inspired by others,
encouragement to soar and chase.

A whole new world without me,
taking it all in with grace.

Hey You, my free spirit
I am here,
as close as I can be,
watching you take flight
in everything you see.

Taking off among your peers,
yearning to be free.
Your world alters to a spectacular, and
more colorful version of me.

Discovering environments,
warming your heart,
some colder.

My teenage child growing
beautifully tall and bolder.

Yes love, it is me, watching your deep breaths
as you take in your passions entirely.

I see your temptation
to sing and dance to every beat.
Your new movements begin
as you prance and twirl
as the music begins to speak.

Your voice, laughter from afar
that we once embraced alone.

Your overnight bags, running out the house
so fast and so grown.

I SEE YOU,
I AM HERE,
IT IS ME....

Always loving you more
than you will ever see.

My child....
Remember the rain, take in the rainbow,
fight for the dance.
Take pause, take a bow, give grace to friendships,
take all the time on romance.

It is now time;
it is time
for your own journey
to begin minus me.

My brave child...
just know that I am there with you always
as close as I can be,
looking through a lens at my child
so beautifully
so wild
so free.

ABOUT THE AUTHOR

Melanie is a proud mother of two who cherishes the moments spent with her family. As her eldest embarks on the journey to college, Melanie has captured the heartwarming milestones of parenthood in this book. Through her writing, she reflects on the love, growth, and memorable moments shared with her children as they journey through life's stages. This book is a tribute to the timeless bond between parents and their children.

Printed in the USA
CPSIA information can be obtained
at www.ICGtesting.com
LVHW070411241124
797348LV00007B/174